MW00993762

_____

_____

_____

_____

DATE

DATE

DATE

DATE

DATE

DATE

DATE

DATE

DATE

DATE

DATE

DATE

DATE

DATE

DATE

DATE

DATE

DATE

DATE

DATE

DATE

DATE

DATE

DATE

DATE

DATE

DATE

DATE

DATE

DATE

DATE

DATE

DATE

DATE

DATE

DATE

DATE

DATE

DATE

DATE

DATE

DATE

DATE

DATE

DATE

DATE

DATE

DATE

DATE

DATE

DATE

DATE

DATE

DATE

DATE

DATE

DATE

DATE

DATE

DATE

DATE

DATE

DATE

DATE

DATE

DATE

DATE

DATE

DATE

DATE

DATE

DATE

DATE

DATE

DATE

DATE

DATE

DATE

DATE

DATE

DATE

DATE

DATE

DATE

DATE

DATE

DATE

DATE

DATE

DATE

DATE

DATE

DATE

DATE

DATE

DATE

DATE

DATE

DATE

DATE

DATE

DATE

DATE

DATE

DATE

DATE

DATE

DATE

DATE

DATE

DATE

DATE

DATE

DATE

DATE

DATE

DATE

DATE

DATE

DATE

DATE

DATE

DATE

DATE

DATE

DATE

DATE

DATE

DATE

DATE

DATE

DATE

DATE

DATE

DATE

DATE

DATE

DATE

DATE

DATE

ABOUT THE ARTIST

Art and animals. These two passions define Dean Russo, a Brooklyn, New York-based artist who uses vibrant Pop Art colors and bold abstract patterns to give a voice to his favorite subject—animals. Dean starts his paintings with the eyes, because, as every animal-lover knows, the eyes are the most expressive. Dean's main subjects are dogs, with pit bulls representing the majority of his work. "Pit bulls are a misunderstood breed, and I'm just happy to be able to get the message about animal rescue out there." Dean Russo Art Studio has a sincere dedication to animal rescue and has participated in charity auctions, donations, and fund-raising events to raise awareness and help out in the animal welfare community. Dean hopes to convey the care and devotion of animal-lovers of every kind, from dogs and cats to horses and beyond. He has a wildlife series in the works, as a way to support the countless animals on the verge of extinction. Through inspiring messages and bright prints, Dean Russo's work is sure to brighten anyone's day. Check out his art at *www.deanrussoart.com.*

MORE JOURNALS FROM DEAN RUSSO

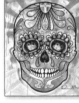    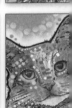

ISBN 978-1-64178-111-4

Fox Chapel Publishing makes every effort to use environmentally friendly paper for printing.

© 2019 by Dean Russo/Artlicensing.com and Quiet Fox Designs, an imprint of Fox Chapel Publishing Company, Inc., 903 Square Street, Mount Jo PA 17552.

We are always looking for talented authors and artists. To submit an idea, please send a brief inquiry to acquisitions@foxchapelpublishing.com.

Printed in Singapore
First printing

Cover background: T30 Gallery/Shutterstock
Endpapers: Tumanyan and Pavlo Chepys/Shutterstock
Page 1: SoulGIE/Shutterstock